MY WEE GRANNY'S SOUPS AND STEWS

Traditional Scottish Recipes
from
My Wee Granny's Table to Yours

Angela Hossack

Copyright © 2019 Angela Hossack

The right of Angela Hossack to be identified as the Author of the Work has been asserted by her in accordance with the Copyright, Designs and Patents Act 1988.

Dedicated to my wee granny –

Annie Clark

1890-1971

Also by Angela Hossack

My Wee Granny's Old Scottish Recipes

My Wee Granny's Bannocks and Bakes

CONTENTS

- Introduction
- It's all about the stock
- Vegetable soups
- Soups made with chicken, mixed fowl or turkey stock
- Soups made with meat stock
- Soups made with rich beef stock
- Soups made with vegetable and lamb stock
- Soups made with ham stock
- Soups made with fish stock
- Vegetable stews
- Chicken stews
- Beef stews
- Lamb stews
- Game stews
- Fish stews

INTRODUCTION

I still make home-made soups and stews because – apart from being filling and wholesome – they are delicious. Generations gone by tended to make a meal in a bowl for economic reasons. Scotland was not a rich nation and Scots tended towards thriftiness so - with large families, a lack of money and with readily available ingredients – children were reared on a variety of soups and men went off to work with their bellies full of the filling stews Scotland has become renowned for.

Sometimes, a bowl or two of soup or stew every day was the mainstay of many a Scottish menu and no child raised with these meals lacked any nutritional need because every food group (except for milk and dairy products) was represented in that one bowl.

My wee granny's recipes have been used across five generations of Scottish women and never a day goes by that my kitchen isn't filled with the aroma of the stockpot. Some of these recipes have been forgotten, or have been adjusted over the years, and it would be lovely to have them resurrected in your kitchens using the original ingredients and methods.

I hope you enjoy reading my wee granny's soup and stew recipes and I hope you try your hand at reproducing them for your family. The recipes are simple to follow and, if you make a large pot, can be easily frozen in small batches.

IT'S ALL ABOUT THE STOCK

First, a word or two about seasoning your stock.

Those of you, who are as old as I am, may remember when everything we ate seemed to be so much tastier than the food we eat now. One of the reasons could be that more salt and more fat was used. Back in the day, there wasn't the health warnings that we're all now used to hearing about reducing our salt and fat intake. We didn't know about cholesterol and high blood pressure and the effects of salt and fat on those conditions, but we know now and, so, we have to look to healthier means of seasoning our stocks.

A little salt and a little fat will continue to be used in my wee granny's stock recipes, but other ingredients – some of which she used and some of which I added to replace the lost salt and fat – have found their way into my stockpots over the years. I've experimented with these ingredients and find that they don't take away from the basic deliciousness of my wee granny's soups and stews.

It goes without saying that you can't make a good pot of soup or stew without a rich base stock. Traditionally, stockpots were on the go all of the time – simmering away over the fire or on the stove with bones and leftovers continuously replenishing it. These days, some home cooks tend to use stock cubes, but I find that relying on cubes alone leads to a soup or stew with very little body.

My wee granny always had her base stocks prepared in advance. I follow in her footsteps and tend to either make my stock the day before I need it or make a huge pot and freeze it.

The most important thing to remember about a good stock is that it needs time... hours and hours of time, but you don't have to stand over it and watch it. You can leave it alone. Just throw your bits and pieces in the pot, cover with water, put a tight lid on and leave it alone for at least four hours, but preferably longer.

Something else that's very important – throw nothing away. Keep and freeze every chicken, turkey and duck carcass. Keep and freeze every trimming from every meat you've used to cook with. Save the lamb bone from the leg you have on Sunday. Oven roast and then keep beef bones, ox tail bones and pork bones. Waste nothing... including skin and fat. If you haven't used the juices from a roast for gravy – don't discard – keep for your stockpot. And, what about the outside celery stalks that you tend to discard, or the stalks of broccoli and cauliflower? The outside leaves and stalks of cabbages? The leftover raw or cooked vegetables? Yes, you've guessed it – throw in the stockpot. Just make sure everything is washed under cold running water first.

Your basic vegetable stock – scrubbed and chopped carrots with their skins left on, the outside celery stalks that you tend to discard, a couple of whole onions, the outside leaves and the end root of the leek (or a whole leek if you have one going spare), cabbage, broccoli and cauliflower stalks, leftover raw and cooked vegetables and a whole garlic bulb (roasted whole first). Use also any leftover salad tomatoes, spring onions (scallions), sweetcorn, peas and peppers. Put everything in a pot with water (The amount of water will depend on how much bits and pieces you've added to the pot, but you must at least ensure everything is covered by water and then add a further 2 cups), put it on to boil, cover with a tight lid, simmer and forget about it.

When it has simmered for at least four hours, carefully drain through a fine colander, ensuring you squeeze out every last bit of stock and then discard the veggie bits and pieces.

Leave the seasoning until after you have drained and sieved through the colander and, this way, you won't lose any of the seasoning with the discarded vegetables. Season to taste with a little salt, white pepper, celery salt, onion salt and (if preferred, a little garlic paste).

I use chicken stock a lot. We eat a lot of chicken in our house and my freezer is usually crammed with carcasses. I have a stock pot that can take up to 8 carcasses.

For added flavour I roast the carcasses in the oven for 30 minutes before throwing them in the stockpot, covering with water, bringing to the boil and simmering under a tight lid for at least 6 hours. I give it a stir now and again and top up with water if necessary, otherwise I leave it alone and get on with other things. Straining can be a bit of a pain, but it's worth it.

Season to taste with salt, white pepper, celery salt and onion salt. I also add a little ground turmeric to my chicken stock.

If possible, make your chicken stock the day before you need it because it is always best refrigerated, and most of the fat then skimmed off the top. It will amaze you just how much fat will float and set on the surface and its then up to you how much of that fat you allow to remain in your stock.

You only actually get about 4 pints of stock from 8 carcasses, but you can imagine how rich and delicious it is.

You can, of course, make smaller amounts of chicken stock. If I know that I want stock for a gravy, or a curry or a small pot of soup or stew the day after I roast a chicken, then I immediately get the carcass on to simmer. A single carcass is simmered for about 3 hours and I get just under a pint of stock.

At Christmas, or other holiday periods, you may have turkey, duck, geese carcasses etc and you can add them to the stockpot with your chicken carcasses to make a mixed fowl stock or – in the case of turkey – make a standalone turkey stock.

Mixed meat stock – made with any or all of your yummy lamb, beef, ox tail and that you have to hand, as well as any meat trimmings or any leftover cooked or uncooked meats. Always roast the bones and trimmings for 30 minutes before adding to your stockpot. Roasting begins the caramelising process and adds a tremendous amount of flavour. Cover with water and bring to the boil. Remove all the scum that forms on the top (this will ensure a nice clear stock).

Gently simmer for as long as you can, but for at least 4 hours. Strain carefully ensuring you get every drop of stock and leave to cool then put in the fridge overnight so that the fat solidifies on top and then skim.

Season to taste with salt, pepper, celery salt and onion salt. I also add a little ground chilli (quarter of a teaspoon) to my mixed meat stock, but this is optional.

Rich beef stock is a bit more expensive to make because it doesn't just rely on bones and trimmings. Hough (shin) and brisket are the staples for a good, rich beef stock along with any beef bones and trimmings, but the meat can then be used for a variety of dishes.

Seal the shin and brisket in a frying pan and add to your stockpot. Roast any beef bones or beef trimmings to hand and then add. Cover with water and bring it to a gentle simmer. After it has simmered for at least 3 hours, remove the shin and the joint of brisket and then continue simmering the bones and trimmings for at least another hour – preferably longer. Season to taste with salt, lots of black pepper, onion salt and celery salt.

Your rich beef stock can be enhanced with the addition of ox tails or you can make a pure Ox tail stock. Ox tails are delicious, and you can use the meaty bones afterwards. Make your ox tail stock as you would a mixed meat or beef stock, remembering to skim off the scum when it comes to the boil. Season to taste.

A favourite stock of my wee granny was a simple vegetable, and breast/neck of lamb stock.

This stock forms the basis of many soups and stews. To the ingredients of the basic vegetable stock, add a roasted breast of lamb and roasted lamb neck bones and follow the method for making the rich beef stock, removing the breast of lamb after 3 hours. Continue to simmer the vegetable and neck bones for a further hour then carefully drain and sieve.

Season to taste with salt, pepper, celery salt and onion salt. Garlic paste and a quarter of a teaspoon of chilli powder can be added, but these are optional.

For Smoked or unsmoked ham stock you need celery stalks, a large leek, a large onion, a couple of carrots and a smoked or unsmoked gammon or ham hock and/or cuts of smoked or unsmoked bacon. Cover with water and bring to a slow boil. Remove the scum formed on the top and simmer for 3 hours. Drain carefully and season to taste with salt, white pepper, celery salt and onion salt. Cool and leave in fridge overnight and skim and discard the fat that has congealed on the top.

Basic fish stock – fish heads and bones fried for a few minutes gently in butter alongside a roughly chopped onion, 2 stalks of roughly chopped celery and roughly chopped stalks of parsley. Season with celery salt, thyme, a bay leaf, salt and pepper then put in your stock pot, add a cup of white wine to every litre of water and simmer for one hour. Strain through a sieve. For a richer shellfish stock use the heads and shells of prawns, lobster shells, razor fish shells and the strained liquor of mussels and follow the method for your basic fish stock but cook out for an additional 30 minutes.

VEGETABLE SOUPS

Kale and Oatmeal Soup

Serves 4

<u>What you will need</u>:
1 litre of vegetable stock
4 cups (chopped) Green kale (240g)
Quarter of a cup of oatmeal (32g)
Half a cup (150ml) double cream

<u>What you need to do:</u>
Wash and de-vein the kale and roughly chop
Bring your vegetable stock to the boil
Add the kale to the stock and simmer for one hour
Remove the kale and chop up finely and toss it in the oatmeal
Return to the pot
Gently warm the cream and add to the pot
Stir and simmer for 5 minutes

Red Lentil and Barley Soup

Serves 6

What you will need:

1.5 litres of vegetable stock

1 cup (128g) of red lentils

1 cup pearl barley

4 carrots

1 onion

2 stalks of celery

2 teaspoons of chopped curly leaf parsley

What you will need to do:

Soak the pearl barley in cold water in the fridge overnight.

Rinse the red lentils and the barley and add to the stock. Bring to the boil, cover with a tight lid and begin simmering.

Peel, chop and dice the carrots and onion and add to the pot.

Remove the fibrous stringy bits from the celery and chop into small pieces and add to the pot and gently simmer for one hour.

Add the parsley just before serving

Tattie (Potato) Soup

Serves 6-8

What you will need:

1.5 litres of vegetable stock

2lb (907g) of potatoes

2 onions

2 stalks of celery

Half a pint (250mls) of milk

Cup of curly leaf parsley

Tablespoon of flour

Splash of vegetable oil

What you will need to do:

Chop and dice the potatoes and onions, remove the fibrous stringy bits of the celery and chop into small pieces. Fry all these vegetables in the vegetable oil for 5 minutes.

Bring the stock to the boil and add the vegetables. Cover and simmer for 15 minutes then use a potato masher to mash.

Wash and chop the parsley.

Blend the flour with the milk and add to the pot to thicken. Stir well and add the parsley.

Tattie (Potato) and Leek Soup

Serves 6-8

What you will need:

1.5 litres of vegetable stock

2lb (907g) potatoes

4 carrots

Small swede

2 leeks

Cup of curly leaf parsley

What you need to do:

Dice the potatoes, swede and 3 of the 4 carrots and add to the vegetable stock. Bring to the boil and simmer for 30 minutes.

Wash and cut the leek lengthways and then into small pieces and after the vegetables have simmered for 30 minutes, add the leek to the pot and simmer for a further 30 minutes.

Chop the curly leaf parsley and add it 5 minutes before serving.

Haricot Bean Soup

Serves 6-8

What you will need:

1.5 litres of vegetable stock

340g (12oz) of pre-soaked haricot beans

2 onions

1 swede

450g (1lb) potatoes

1 tablespoon of flour

2 cups of milk

Half a cup of curly leaf parsley

What you will need to do:

Cut and dice the onions, swede and potatoes. Rinse the beans and add to the stock along with the diced vegetables. Bring to the boil and cover with a tight lid.

Simmer for 2 hours then force through a sieve and return to the pot. Mix the flour with a little of the milk and stir through the soup to thicken and then add the remaining milk.

Chop the parsley and just before serving, add to the pot.

Tomato Soup

Serves 4

<u>What you will need:</u>

1 litre of vegetable stock

8 large or 10 medium blanched and skinned tomatoes

1 carrot

1 onion

2 tablespoons of sago

2 cups of milk

<u>What you will need to do</u>:

Cut up tomatoes, onion and carrot and add to the stock in a pot. Bring to the boil and add the sago. Simmer for 30 minutes. Pass through a sieve, return to the pot and add the milk. Stir and heat, but do not boil.

Tomato, Red Pepper and Lentil Soup

Serves 4

What you will need:

1 litre of vegetable stock

6 medium blanched and skinned tomatoes

2 red peppers

1 onion

2 cloves of garlic

2 teaspoons of olive oil

Half a cup (60g) of red lentils

What you will need to do:

Quarter the tomatoes, peppers and onion and put on a baking tray with the garlic

Mix the vegetables with the olive oil and roast in a medium oven for 15-20 minutes

Squeeze the roasted garlic from their skins and mix through the roasted vegetables. Remove the pepper skins

Rinse the lentils and add to the stock, bring to a simmer and simmer for 15 minutes, stirring occasionally

Add the vegetables and simmer for a further 10 minutes

Cream of Mushroom Soup

Serves 4

What you will need:

1 litre of vegetable stock

500g of mixed mushrooms

50g of butter

1 onion

1 cup of crème fraiche

2 tablespoons of cream

What you will need to do:

Chop the mushrooms and the onion and fry in the butter until soft

Add to the stock and bring to a simmer then simmer for 20 minutes

Stir in the crème fraiche and simmer for a further 5 minutes

Blend (blitz) the soup and serve topped with a swirl of cream

Spicy Parsnip Soup

Serves 4

<u>What you will need</u>:

1 litre of vegetable stock

1 cup of cream

Half a teaspoon of smoked paprika

Half a teaspoon of cumin

Half a teaspoon of chopped ginger

A quarter of a teaspoon of chili powder

6 large parsnips

1 onion

2 cloves of garlic

Knob of butter

Handful of coriander leaves

<u>What you will need to do</u>:

Peel and chop the parsnips and slice the garlic

Add to the butter in a frying pan and fry gently for a few minutes then add the chopped parsnip, the smoked paprika, cumin and chili powder

Fry gently for a few minutes then add to the vegetable stock and simmer for 30 minutes then stir in most of the cream

Blend (blitz) thoroughly until smooth and serve with a swirl of cream and with a garnish of chopped coriander leaves

Spicy Vegetable Soup

Serves 4

What you will need:

1 litre of vegetable stock (you may need to add more later)

1 cup of milk

2 carrots

2 potatoes

2 small white turnips

1 parsnip

Half a cup of green lentils

1 onion

Half a teaspoon of cumin

Half a teaspoon of smoked paprika

Half a teaspoon of chili powder

Knob of butter

What you will need to do:

Peel and chop all the vegetables and fry off with the knob of butter then add to the vegetable stock and bring to a simmer. Add the spices and then simmer for 15 minutes

Rinse and then add the lentils and simmer for a further 30 minutes then add the milk and blend (blitz) thoroughly. Add more stock if required.

Potato and Mint Pea Soup

Serves 4

<u>What you will need:</u>

1 litre of vegetable stock

4 large potatoes

1 onion

3 cups of frozen peas

Knob of butter

2 tablespoons of cream

<u>What you will need to do:</u>

Peel and chop the onion and potatoes and fry off with the butter for 5 minutes

Add to the stock and bring to a simmer

Simmer for 20 minutes and then blend (blitz) thoroughly

Serve with a swirl of cream

Carrot and Ginger Soup

Serves 4

What you will need:

1 litre of vegetable stock

6 carrots

1 onion

2 tablespoons of grated ginger

2 tablespoons of cream

Half a teaspoon of cayenne pepper

Knob of butter

What you will need to do:

Peel and chop the carrots and the onion and fry off for a couple of minutes with the butter then add the grated ginger and the cayenne pepper and fry for another minute.

Add to the stock and bring to a simmer then simmer for 15 minutes and then add the cream blend (blitz) thoroughly with the cream

SOUPS MADE WITH CHICKEN, MIXED FOWL OR TURKEY STOCK

Cock-a-leekie Soup

Serves 6-8

<u>What you will need</u>:

1.5 litres of chicken stock

1 small chicken

8 leeks

<u>What you will need to do:</u>

Bring the stock to a slow simmer and add the chicken to the pot.

Wash the leeks and prepare them by cutting off the root and about an inch from the top; remove the outer leaf and cut/split lengthwise then chop into one-inch lengths. Give the cut leeks a final rinse in cold water and add to the pot.

Simmer for one hour. Remove the chicken and take it off the bone and return the chicken meat to the pot. Remove from the heat and serve.

Feather Fowlie

Serves 6-8

What you will need:

1.5 litres of chicken stock

Small chicken

2 slices of ham

Head of celery

2 onions

3 egg yolks

Half a cup of curly leaf parsley

A teaspoon of thyme

A dessertspoon of cream

What you need to do:

Joint the chicken and add it to the stock with the 2 slices of ham and bring to the boil. Simmer for 40 minutes. Remove the fibrous stringy bits from the celery and cut into small pieces. Chop and dice the onions, chop the parsley and add to the pot with the thyme and simmer for a further 20 minutes.

Remove the chicken and the ham Take the meat off the bone and cut into small pieces. Cut the ham into small pieces. Skim the grease from the stock. Remove the pot from the heat and stir in three whisked egg yolks and the dessertspoon of warmed cream. Add the chopped chicken and ham meat.

Chicken Soup

Serves 4

<u>What you will need</u>:

1 litre of chicken stock

2 chicken legs

1 leek

2 large carrots

Half a cup (170g) of rice

Half a cup of curly leaf parsley

<u>What you will need to do</u>:

Put the chicken into the stock, bring to the boil and simmer for 10 minutes.

Cut and finely dice the carrot and add to the pot. Cut the leek lengthways and then cut into small pieces. Add to the pot with the rice and simmer for a further 30 minutes.

Add more stock if required.

Remove the chicken and take the meat off the bone and return to the pot.

Chop and add the parsley 5 minutes before serving.

Chunky Chicken and Vegetable soup

Serves 6-8

What you will need:

1.5 litres of chicken stock

2 chicken legs

1 large leek

2 large carrots

1 potato

2 white turnips

1 parsnip

Half a small swede

Small head of broccoli

Half a cup of curly leaf parsley

What you will need to do:

Put the chicken into the stock, bring to the boil and simmer for 10 minutes.

Peel, rinse and cut up all of the vegetables and add to the pot. Simmer for a further 30 minutes.

Remove the chicken and take the meat off the bone and return to the pot.

Chop and add the parsley 5 minutes before serving.

Cream of Chicken Soup

Serves 4

<u>What you will need:</u>

1 litre of chicken stock

2 chicken legs

1 large onion

1 medium leek

1 potato

2 stalks of celery

2 large carrots

Half a cup of flat leaf parsley

Knob of butter

Half a cup of cream

<u>What you will need to do:</u>

Put the chicken into the stock, bring to the boil and simmer for 10 minutes.

Cut the leek lengthways and then cut into small pieces. Peel and chop the onion. Remove the fibrous, stringy bits from the celery and chop. Peel and cube the potato.

Fry off all the vegetables with the butter for 5 minutes and then add to the stock. Simmer for a further 30 minutes.

Remove the chicken and then blend (blitz) the soup. Take off the heat and stir in the cream. Finely chop the chicken and add to the pot. Serve with a garnish of finely chopped parsley.

Chicken Broth

Serves 8-10

What you will need:

2 litres of chicken stock

2 chicken legs

Quarter of a cup of split yellow peas

Quarter of a cup of split green peas

One cup of white rice

Quarter of a cup of red lentils

1 large leek

2 large carrots

Half a cup of curly leaf parsley

What you will need to do:

Pre-soak the peas in cold water overnight.

Put the chicken into the stock, bring to the boil and simmer for 10 minutes.

Cut and finely dice the carrot and add to the pot. Cut the leek lengthways and then cut into small pieces. Add to the pot with the pre-soaked peas and the rice and simmer for a further 40 minutes.

Remove the chicken and take the meat off the bone, chop finely and return to the pot. Chop and add the parsley 5 minutes before serving.

Turkey Broth

Serves 6-8

What you will need:

1.5 litres of turkey stock

500g of cooked leftover holiday turkey

Quarter of a cup of split yellow peas

Quarter of a cup of split green peas

Half of a cup of pearl barley

Half of a cup of red lentils

1 large leek

2 large carrots

Half a cup of curly leaf parsley

What you will need to do:

Pre-soak the peas and the barley overnight in cold water

Peel and finely dice the carrots and wash and finely chop up the leek then add to the stock and bring to a rolling simmer. Rinse and add the peas and the barley and simmer for 10 minutes and then add the lentils. Simmer for a further 30 minutes and then add the leftover turkey that you have diced.

Chop the parsley and add just before serving

Spicy Turkey Soup

Serves 4-6

<u>What you will need:</u>

1 litre of turkey stock

250g of leftover turkey

1 red pepper

1 large carrot

1 large potato

2 small white turnips

1 parsnip

Half a cup of green lentils

1 onion

Half a teaspoon of cumin

Half a teaspoon of smoked paprika

Half a teaspoon of chili powder

Knob of butter

<u>What you will need to do</u>:

Peel and dice all the vegetables and fry off with the knob of butter then add to the turkey stock and bring to a simmer. Add the spices and then simmer for 15 minutes

Rinse and add the green lentils and simmer for a further 30 minutes. Chop and add the turkey and simmer for another 5 minutes. Add more stock if required.

Duck Broth

Serves 4-6

<u>What you will need</u>:

1 litre of mixed fowl or chicken stock

250g of leftover duck

2 brown onions

1 stick of celery

200g of mushrooms

Sprig of thyme

1 bay leaf

2 carrots

200mls of sherry

<u>What you will need to do:</u>

Peel and finely dice the onions and carrots. Remove fibrous bits from the celery stalk and finely dice. Finely dice the mushrooms.

Add the onions, carrots and celery to the stock. Add the thyme and the bay leaf and gently simmer for 15 minutes then add the mushrooms, the duck and the sherry and simmer for a further 5 minutes. Remove the sprig of thyme and the bay leaf.

SOUPS MADE WITH MEAT STOCK

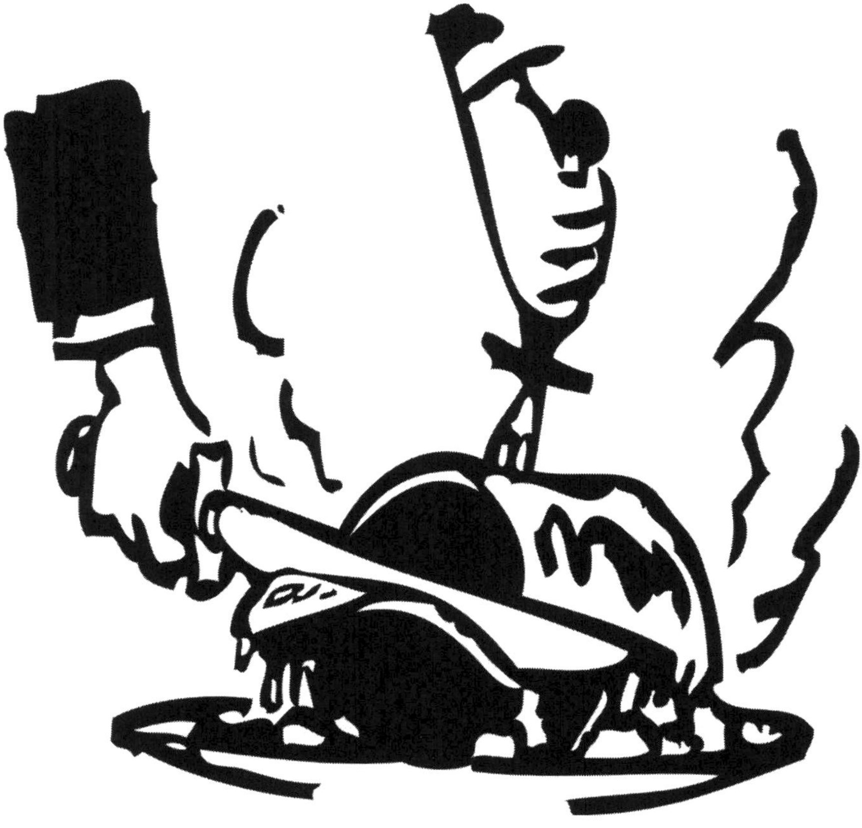

Beef, Pea and Barley Soup

Serves 4-6

<u>What you will need:</u>

1 litre of rich beef stock

1 cup of pearl barley

1 onion

Half a cup of frozen green peas

More stock if required

<u>What you will need to do</u>:

Pre-soak the pearl barley in cold water overnight

Peel and finely dice the onion and add to the stock then add the barley and simmer for 30 minutes

Add more stock if required

Add the peas and simmer for a further 5 minutes

Lamb and Cabbage Soup

Serves 4-6

<u>What you will need</u>:

1 litre of the vegetable and lamb stock

Leftover lamb

2 stalks of celery

A quarter of a green cabbage

2 tomatoes

1 leek

2 carrots

<u>What you need to do</u>:

Remove the fibrous, stringy bits from the celery and finely dice.

Chop up the cabbage and peel and finely dice the carrots. Roughly chop the tomatoes and wash and chop the leek

Add everything to the stock and simmer for 15 minutes then add the leftover lamb

Scotch Broth

Serves 6 - 8

<u>What you will need</u>:

1.5 litres of the vegetable and lamb stock

The breast of lamb used for the stock

Pre-soaked broth mixture – (64g of pearl barley, 64g of yellow split peas and 64g of green split peas)

2 large onions

4 large carrots

2 white turnips

Small swede

A head of celery

A cup of chopped curly leaf parsley (128g)

<u>What you need to do</u>:

Add the pre-soaked broth mix to the stock and bring to a slow boil. Simmer for forty minutes, stirring occasionally.

Chop and dice the onions, carrots, turnips and celery and add to the pot. Continue to simmer for a further fifteen minutes then add most of the parsley and the lamb and simmer for a further five minutes. Take off the heat and chop the lamb and add to the pot with the remaining parsley.

Skink

Serves 6-8

What you will need:

1.5 litres of rich beef stock

The shin and/or the brisket used to make the stock

4 large carrots

1 small swede

2 leeks

Head of celery

2 onions

Half of a savoy cabbage

What you need to do:

Bring stock to a slow simmer

Chop and dice the carrots, swede and onions

Chop and cut up the celery

Cut the cabbage and the leeks and chop into small pieces

Add all of the prepared vegetables to the stock and simmer for 30 minutes.

Cut the shin and/or brisket into small cubes and add to the pot.

Switch off and allow the residual heat to warm through the beef.

This is a thick soup, but you can add more stock if you want it a little thinner.

Oxtail Soup

Serves 4

What you will need:

1 litre of your oxtail stock

8 pieces of the pre-cooked oxtail used to make your stock

3 carrots

1 swede

2 white turnips

1 large onion

Tablespoon of vegetable oil

What you will need to do:

Chop and dice the carrots, swede, turnips and onion and fry off for a few minutes in the vegetable oil.

Bring the stock to a slow simmer, add the vegetables and simmer for 30 minutes.

Add the oxtails to the soup to warm through.

Serve 2 portions of the oxtails with each portion of soup (this was my wee granny's preferred way to serve the oxtails, as sucking out the meat from the bones was awesome, but you can fork the meat out of the bones and add it to the soup if you prefer.)

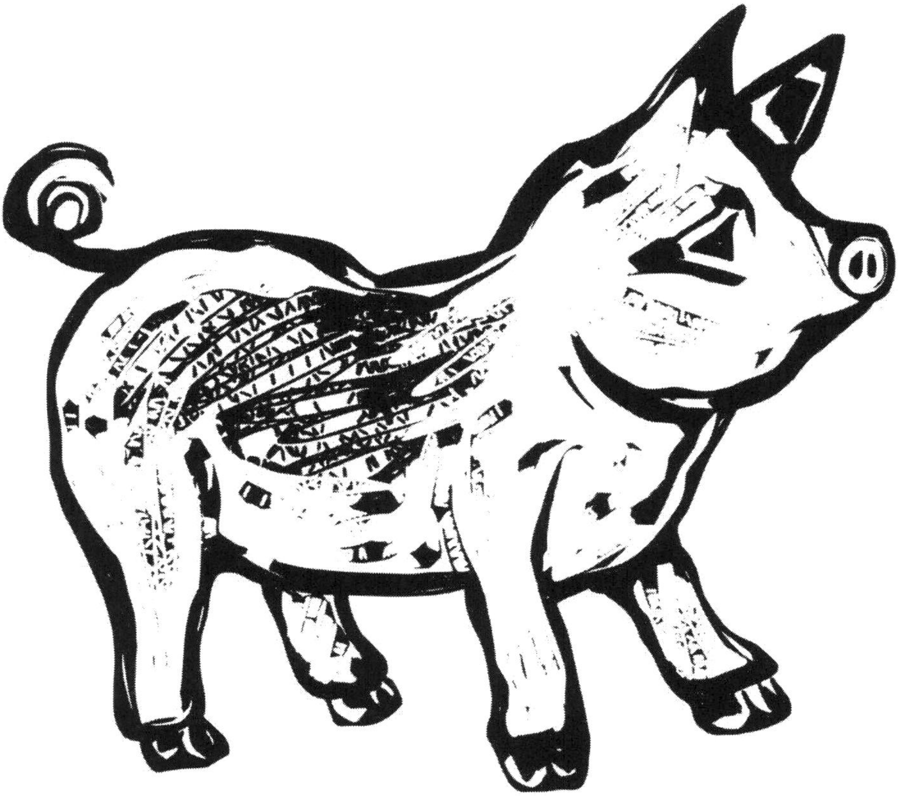

SOUPS MADE WITH HAM STOCK

Red Lentil and Tomato Soup

Serves 4

What you will need:

A third of a litre of slightly salted water

1 litre of ham stock

1 cup (128g) of red lentils

4 carrots

1 onion

2 stalks of celery

4 large fresh tomatoes

What you will need to do:

Bring the salted water to the boil

Rinse the red lentils and add to the water. Cover and simmer for 20 minutes stirring frequently so as not to burn on the bottom. Add more boiling water if required.

Peel, chop and dice the carrots, onion and the tomatoes.

Remove the fibrous stringy bits from the celery and chop into small pieces.

In a separate pot, bring the stock to the boil, add all of the vegetables and simmer for 20 minutes.

After the lentils have simmered for 20 minutes leave to one side.

Once the vegetables have simmered in the stock for 20 minutes, use a potato masher to roughly mash them and then add the lentils. Stir thoroughly and simmer for a further 10 minutes.

Dried Pea and Ham Soup

Serves 4

What you will need:

1 litre of ham stock

225g (8oz) of pre-soaked dried green peas

1 onion

1 small white turnip

Half a cup of curly leaf parsley

Teaspoon of vegetable oil

What you will need to do:

Chop and dice the onion, carrot and turnip and fry gently in the oil then add to the stock with the peas. Bring to the boil, cover and simmer for 2 hours.

Chop the parsley for garnish

Cream of Ham and Vegetable Soup

Serves 4

What you will need:

1 litre of ham stock

Leftover ham

1 celery stalk

4 red potatoes

1 red onion

1 carrot

1 tin of evaporated milk

Knob of butter

Tablespoon of flour

What you will need to do:

Peel and finely dice the potatoes, onion and carrot

Remove the fibrous, stringy bits from the celery and finely dice

Dust all of the vegetables in the flour and gently fry off in the butter then add to the broth and simmer for 20 minutes

Add the evaporated milk and stir through until completely mixed and then add the leftover ham and simmer for a further 5 minutes

Ham and Potato Soup

Serves 4

What you will need:

1 litre of ham stock

Leftover ham

2 celery stalks

4 red potatoes

1 red onion

1 carrot

1 parsnip

2 tablespoons of cream

1 sprig of thyme

1 bay leaf

Knob of butter

What you will need to do:

Peel and cube the potatoes, carrot, parsnip and onions. Remove the fibrous, stringy bits from the celery and chop.

Fry all of the vegetable in the butter for 5 minutes and add to the stock along with the sprig of thyme and the bay leaf. Simmer for 20 minutes and then remove half of the vegetables.

Remove the thyme and the bay leaf

Blend (blitz) the remaining vegetables with the stock and then return the remaining vegetables to the pot along with the leftover ham and stir in the cream

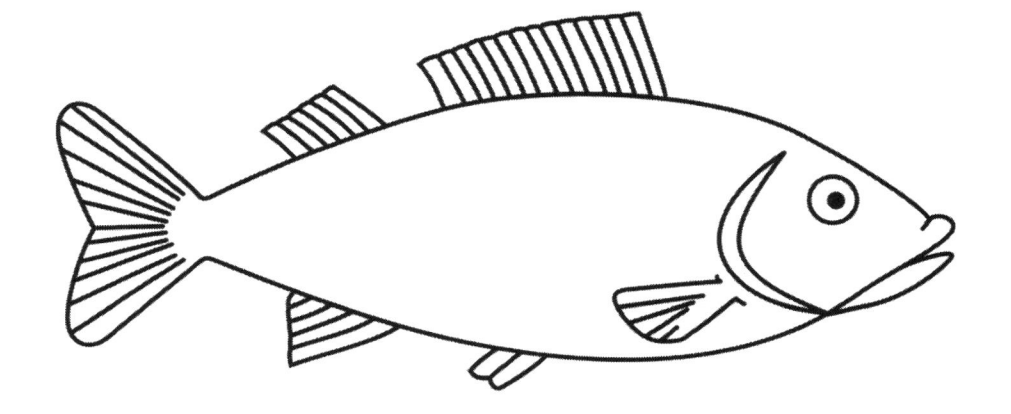

SOUPS MADE WITH FISH STOCK

Cullen Skink

Serves 4-6

What you will need:

(There is no need to use fish stock with this recipe)

2 large pieces of smoked haddock (undyed)

1 onion

2 knobs of butter

2 cups of milk

1 cup of cream

4 potatoes

1 bay leaf

Half a cup of parsley

What you will need to do

Put the haddock in a large pan and cover with the milk (add more milk if needed to just cover the fish. Add the bay leaf and bring to a gentle simmer and then simmer for 10 minutes

Peel and chop the onion and fry until soft in the butter

Remove the fish from the pan and put to the side until later

Peel and cube the potatoes and add to the milk liquor then simmer until potatoes are cooked then remove the bay leaf, add the cream and onions. Chop the parsley and add. Simmer for a further minute

Shell Fish Soup

Serves 4-6

What you will need:

1 litre of rich shellfish stock

100g Clams

100g Cockles

100g Mussels

4 Razor fish

100g King prawns

1 cup of milk

Knob of butter

Half a cup of oatmeal

What you will need to do:

Put all the shellfish, except the prawns, in a pot, cover with water and bring to the boil. Simmer until cooked and remove any where the shells have remained closed.

Shell and de-vein the king prawns.

Remove all the shellfish and remove from the shells. Cut up the razor fish and then add the clams, mussels and razor fish to your prepared stock. Bring back to a gentle simmer, add the half cup of oatmeal, the knob of butter and the cup of milk. After five minutes add the de-shelled and de-veined prawns. Switch off the heat, cover and let stand until the prawns cook in the residual heat.

Partan Bree (Crab Soup)

Serves 4-6

What you will need:

Half a litre of shellfish stock

1 large crab

A quarter of a cup of rice

Two and a half cups of milk

Three quarters of a cup of cream

One tablespoon of chives

What you will need to do:

Cook the crab and remove the meat, separating the brown and white meat

Cook the rice in the stock and the milk, add the brown meat and blend (blitz)

Add the white meat and mix through the cream

Garnish with chopped chives

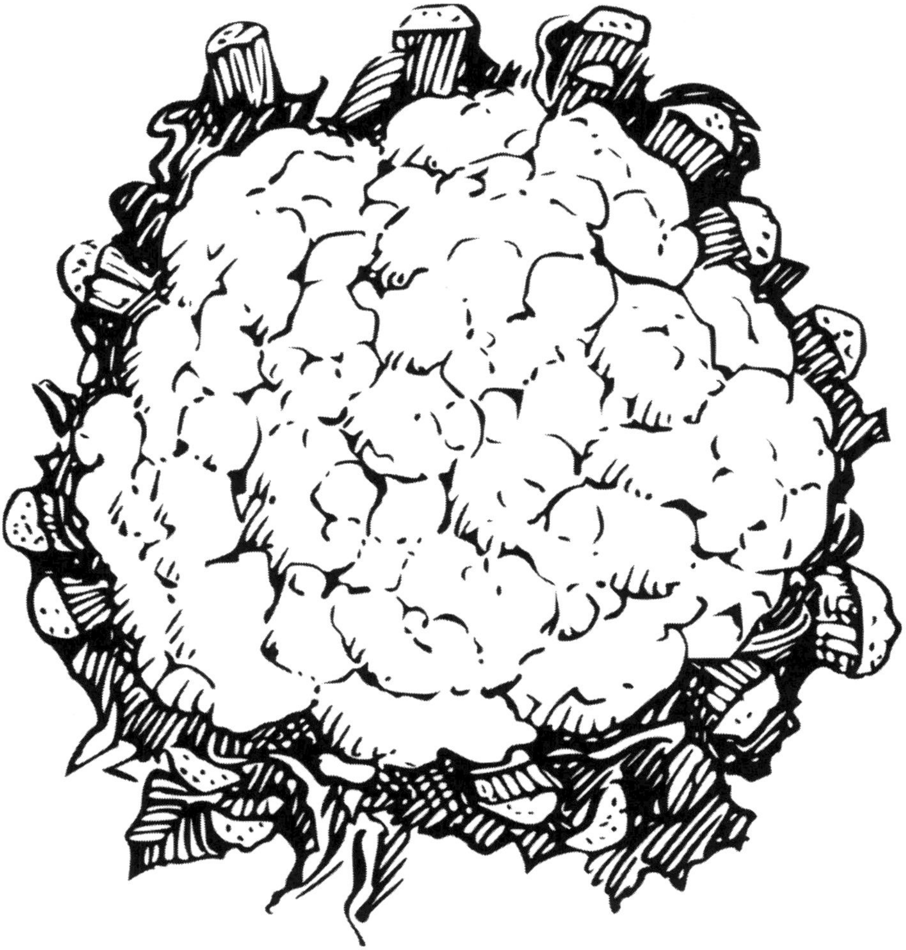

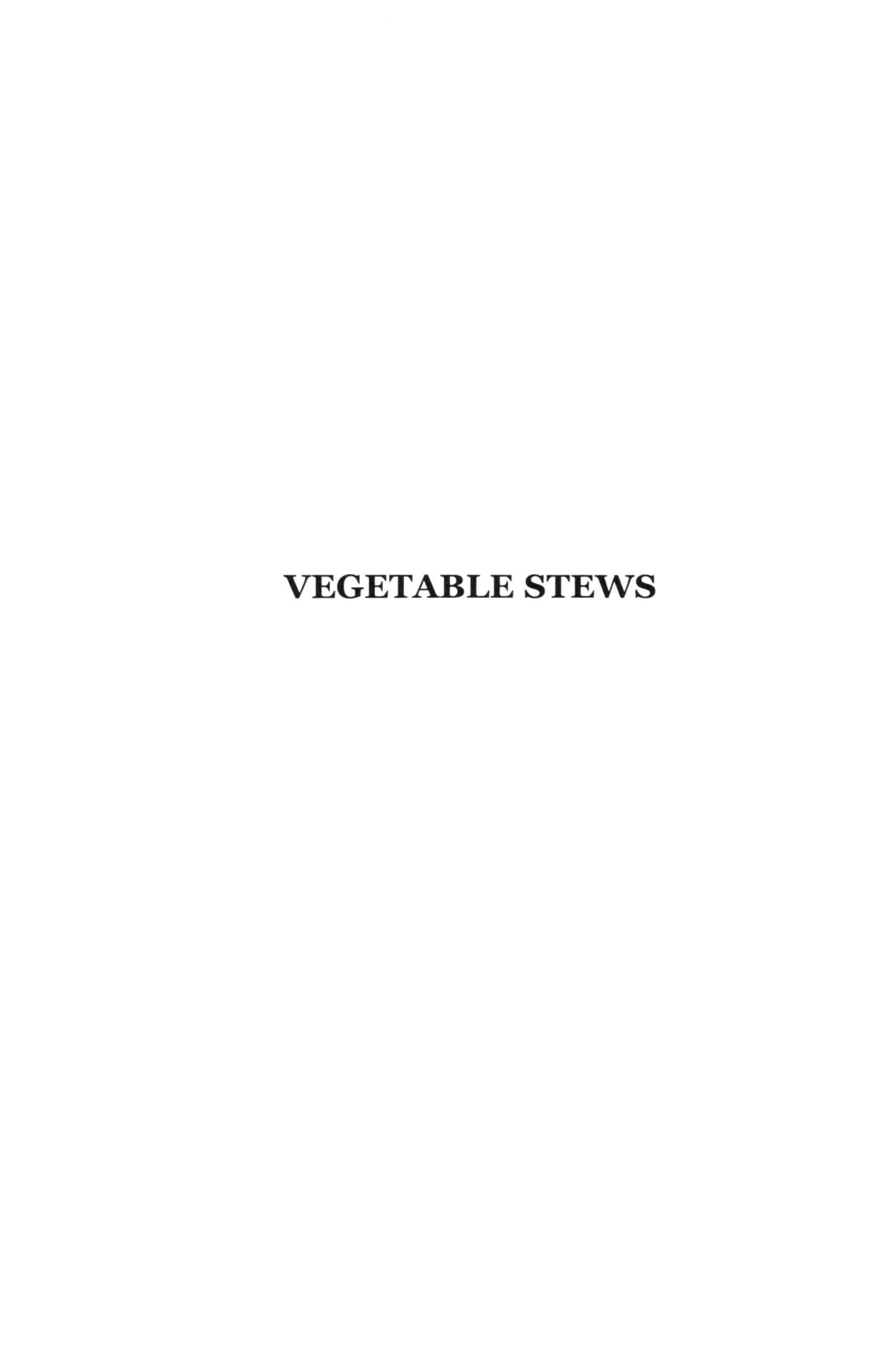

VEGETABLE STEWS

Vegetable Hotch Potch

Serves 6-8

What you will need:

1 litres of vegetable stock

6 carrots

6 small white turnips

1 cup (128g) of dried peas

1 cup (128g) of broad beans

Small cauliflower

1 little gem lettuce

6 spring onions

Half a cup (65g) of curly leaf parsley

What you need to do:

Skin half of the peas and all of the broad beans and then   put half of the peas to one side

Bring stock to the boil and add the skinned peas and broad beans

Peel, cut and dice the carrots and the turnips and add to the pot then simmer for 40 minutes

Meantime cut the cauliflower into florets and chop the lettuce. Cut the spring onions into small pieces. Chop the curly leaf parsley. After the initial 40 minutes simmer, add the remaining half cup of peas, the cauliflower, lettuce and spring onions to the pot. Stir and then add the chopped parsley. This is a thick soup, but you can add more stock if you prefer it a little thinner.

Spicy Green Vegetable Stew

Serves 6-8

<u>What you will need</u>:

1 litre of vegetable stock

200 grams of green beans

200 grams of broad beans

Half a cup of frozen green peas

200 grams of broccoli

2 stalks of celery

Half a teaspoon of smoked paprika

Half a teaspoon of cumin

Half a teaspoon of chopped ginger

A quarter of a teaspoon of chili powder

Half a cup of green lentils

Knob of butter

<u>What you need to do</u>:

De-shell the broad beans. Remove the fibrous, stringy bits from the celery and finely chop. Wash and chop the green beans and wash and cut the broccoli into florets

Fry off the celery with the butter

Add the broad beans, green beans, peas and lentils to the stock and bring to a gentle simmer and add the celery and the spices. Simmer for 30 minutes

White Bean Stew

Serves 6-8

What you will need:

1 litre of vegetable stock

400g of haricot beans

400g of chick peas

1 onion

2 sticks of celery

2 carrots

Half a cup of parsley

2 cloves of garlic

Knob of butter

What you need to do:

Chop the onions. Remove the fibrous, stringy bits from the celery. Finely dice the carrots and chop the garlic. Fry the onions, garlic and the celery in the butter until soft.

Add the haricot beans and chick peas to the stock and bring to a gentle simmer then add the onions, garlic and celery.

Chop the parsley and add to the pot and simmer for a further minute.

Spicy Cauliflower and Potato Stew

Serves 6-8

What you will need:

1 litre of vegetable stock

1 large cauliflower

3 large potatoes

1 onion

2 stalks of celery

Half a teaspoon of smoked paprika

Half a teaspoon of cumin

Half a teaspoon of chopped ginger

A quarter of a teaspoon of chili powder

1 cup of cream

Knob of butter

What you need to do:

Dice the onion. Remove the fibrous, stringy bits from the celery and chop. Peel and dice the potatoes and cut the cauliflower into florets.

Fry off the onion and celery in the butter for a couple of minutes and add to the stock in a pot then add the potatoes, cauliflower and spices. Gently simmer for 20 minutes and then stir in the cream and simmer for a further minute

Barley and Root Vegetable Stew

Serves 6-8

What you will need:

1.5 litres of vegetable stock

3 large potatoes

Half a swede

3 large carrots

1 parsnip

1 cup of pearl barley

Half a cup of parsley

What you need to do:

Pre-soak the barley overnight in cold water, rinse and add to the stock. Bring to a simmer and simmer for 15 minutes.

Peel and dice the potatoes, carrots, swede and parsnip and add to the pot. Simmer for a further 20 minutes

Finely chop the parsley and add to the post before serving

Quick and Easy Chili Bean and Tomato Stew

Serves 4-6

<u>What you will need</u>:

Half a litre of vegetable stock

4 large tomatoes

1 tin of chick peas

1 tin of kidney beans

1 onion

One teaspoon of chilli powder (or to preference)

Half a teaspoon of celery salt

Half a teaspoon of garlic salt

Teaspoon of vegetable oil

<u>What you need to do:</u>

Blanche and skin the tomatoes and quarter

Chop the onion and fry off in vegetable oil with the chilli

Add the tomatoes, chick peas, kidney beans and onions to the stock and simmer for 10 minutes

Mixed Lentil and Root Vegetable Stew

Serves 6-8

<u>What you will need</u>:

1.5 litres of vegetable stock

Half a cup of red lentils

A third of a cup of pay lentils

3 potatoes

Half of a swede

2 large carrots

1 parsnip

<u>What you need to do:</u>

Rinse and add the lentils to half of the stock and bring to a rolling simmer. Simmer for 10 minutes, stirring a few times.

Peel and cut into chunks the potatoes, swede and parsnip

Add the remaining stock to the pot alongside the vegetables, stir and simmer for a further 20 minutes

Barley and Root Vegetable Stew

Serves 6-8

<u>What you will need</u>:

1 litre of vegetable stock

3 large potatoes

Half a swede

3 large carrots

1 parsnip

1 cup of pearl barley

Half a cup of parsley

<u>What you need to do</u>:

Pre-soak the barley overnight, add to the stock and simmer for 15 minutes

Peel, chop and dice the potatoes, swede, carrots and parsnip and add to the pot along with the remaining stock

Simmer for a further 20 minutes

Finely chop the parsley and add just before serving

CHICKEN STEWS

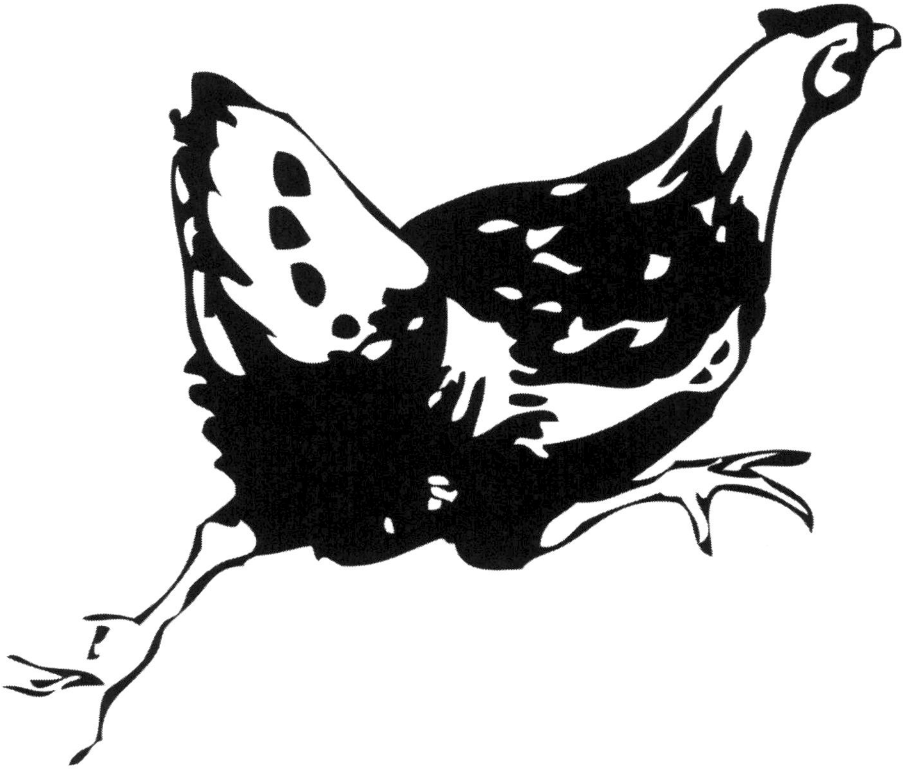

Basic Chicken Stew

Serves 6-8

What you will need:

2 cups of chicken stock

1 cup of dry white wine

8 chicken thigh fillets

2 tablespoons butter

2 large onions

3 carrots

2 sprigs thyme

4 potatoes

1 cup of parsley

What you will need to do:

Fry the chicken in the butter until browned

Peel and finely dice the onions, carrots and potatoes and add to the pot. Add the sprigs of thyme, mix thoroughly and then add the chicken stock. Cover and simmer for 40 minutes, remove the thyme and add the white wine.

Finely chop the parsley, add to the pot, mix and simmer for a further 5 minutes. Thicken with flour or corn flour (corn starch)

Chicken, Mushroom and Port Stew

Serves 4-6

<u>What you will need:</u>

1 whole chicken

Half a litre of chicken stock

1 cup of port

200g of mushrooms

2 tablespoons butter

<u>What you will need to do</u>:

Joint the chicken and brown in the butter

Chop the mushrooms and add to the pot and continue frying for a few minutes then add the stock.

Cover and simmer for 40 minutes then add the port.

Simmer for a further 10 minutes. Thicken with flour or corn flour (corn starch)

Chicken, Chicken Liver and Onion Stew

Serves 4

What you will need:

Half a litre of chicken stock

4 skinned chicken thighs

150g of chicken livers

2 onions

1 stick of celery

Knob of butter

What you will need to do:

Peel and dice the onions. Remove the fibrous, stringy bits from the celery and finely chop and then fry until soft in the butter. Chop the chicken livers and add to the pot and fry for a minute

Add the chicken thighs and the stock, cover and simmer for 40 minutes. Thicken with flour or corn flour (corn starch)

Chicken and Butterbean Stew

Serves 4

What you will need:

2 cups of chicken stock

1 large tin of butterbeans

4 skinned chicken thighs

2 stalks of celery

4 shallots

1 teaspoon of paprika

2 tablespoons of tomato puree

Knob of butter

What you will need to do:

peel and chop the shallots. Remove the fibrous stringy bits from the celery and chop then fry off in the butter and the paprika with the onions for a few minutes then add the tomato puree

add the chicken thighs and cover with the stock and simmer for 40 minutes

Add the butterbeans and simmer for a further 5 minutes

Spicy Chicken and Tomato Stew

Serves 4

<u>What you will need</u>:

2 cups of chicken stock

4 chicken thighs

6 tomatoes

1 tablespoon of tomato puree

Half a teaspoon of cumin

Half a teaspoon of smoked paprika

Half a teaspoon of chilli powder

4 skinned chicken thighs

2 stalks of celery

2 onions

Knob of butter

<u>What you will need to do</u>:

Peel and chop the onions. Remove the fibrous stringy bits from the celery and chop. Fry the onions and the celery in the butter with the spices for a few minutes Add the stock, the tomato puree and the chicken thighs, cover and simmer for 40 minutes

Blanche and quarter the tomatoes and add to the pot with the tomato puree and simmer for a further 10 minutes

BEEF STEWS

Stew and Dook

Serves 6-8

This stew is not served browned nor thickened.

What you will need:

1 litre of rich beef stock

1200g (3lbs) beef Hough (shin)

250g of minced beef

3 beef kidneys

6 onions

What you will need to do:

Remove the fat from the Hough (shin) and cube

Chop and dice the onions

Cut the kidneys length ways and remove as much of the fat gristle from the middle. Chop.

Bring the stock to a gentle boil and add the cubed Hough, the minced beef, the diced onions and the kidneys.

Simmer very gently for 3 hours and add additional salt and black pepper if required

Serve in a bowl and then dook (dip) in your bread

Beef and Pickled Walnut Stew

Serves 4-6

What you will need:

500mls of rich beef stock

500g of shin

200g of pickled walnuts

200mls of port

Handful of parsley

2 onions

1 tablespoon of flour

2 knobs of butter of butter

What you will need to do:

Chop and dice the onions. Cut the walnuts in half

Cube the shin dip in the flour and then brown in a pan with one knob of butter. When brown add to the stock, cover and simmer for 2 hours.

Fry the onions with the second knob of butter until browned and soft and then add to the stock with the pickled walnuts and the port and simmer for a further 30 minutes

Chop the parsley and add to the pot before serving

Thicken with flour or corn flour (corn starch)

Oxtail Stew

Serves 4

What you will need:

500mls of rich beef stock

1 whole ox tail

2 carrots

2 onions

1 tablespoon of flour

I tablespoon of butter

What you will need to do:

Chop and dice the carrots and onions.

Remove excess fa and cut the ox tail into joints. Dip in the flour and brown in a pan with the butter. When brown add to the stock, cover and simmer for 2 hours then add the vegetables and simmer for a further 30 minutes.

Thicken with flour or corn flour (corn starch)

Everyday Beef Stew

Serves 6-8

What you will need:

500mls of rich beef stock

1kg of beef shin

4 carrots

3 onions

2 parsnips

6 small white turnips

1 tablespoon of flour

I tablespoon of butter

What you will need to do:

Chop and dice the carrots, parsnips, turnips and onions

Cube the shin and dip in the flour and brown in a pan with the butter. When brown add the stock and simmer for 2 hours.

After 2 hours, add the vegetables and cover and simmer for a further 30 minutes

Thicken with flour or corn flour (corn starch)

Beef Stew with Potatoes and Swede

Serves 4

What you will need:

500mls of rich beef stock

500g of beef shin

1 small swede (approx. 500g)

2 onions

1 stick of celery

4 large potatoes

200mls of red wine

1 tablespoon of flour

Knob of butter

What you will need to do:

Remove the fibrous, stringy bitts from the celery and chop. Peel and dice the swede, potatoes and onions

Dice the beef shin and coat in the flour and fry until browned in the butter and then add to the stock, cover and simmer for 2 hours.

After 2 hours, add the diced vegetables and the wine to the pan and cook for a further 30 minutes

Thicken with flour or corn flour (corn starch)

Spicy Minced Beef Stew

Serves 4

What you will need:

500mls of rich beef stock

500g of minced beef

2 carrots

2 onions

1 celery stalk

Half a teaspoon of cumin

Half a teaspoon of smoked paprika

Half a teaspoon of chilli powder

2 large tomatoes

I tablespoon of butter

What you will need to do:

Dice the onions

Brown the minced beef and the diced onions in the butter along with the spices

Remove the fibrous, stringy bits from the celery, chop and add to the mince and onions

Peel and dice the carrots, blanche the tomatoes and roughly chop then add to the pot along with the stock

Cover and simmer for 1 hour

Thicken with flour or corn flour (corn starch)

Beef Stew and Butterbeans

Serves 8

What you will need:

1 litre of rich beef stock

500g of minced beef

500g of shin

2 onions

400g of butterbeans

Knob of butter

Tablespoon of flour

What you will need to do:

Dice the onions

Dice the shin and coat in the flour. Mix through the minced beef and add the onions then brown off in the butter

Add to the stock, cover and simmer for 2 hours then add a 400g tin of butterbeans and simmer for a further 30 minutes.

Thicken with flour or corn flour (corn starch)

Mixed Bean and Beef Stew

Serves 8-10

<u>What you will need</u>:

1.5 litres of rich beef stock

500g of minced beef

500g of shin

2 onions

200g of butterbeans

200g of haricot beans

200g chick peas

200g of red kidney beans

Knob of butter

Tablespoon of flour

Flour or cornflour (corn flour) to thicken

<u>What you will need to do</u>:

Dice the onions

Dice the shin and coat in the flour. Mix through the minced beef and add the onions then brown off in the butter

Add to the stock, cover and simmer for 2 hours then add the butterbeans, haricot beans, chick peas and red kidney beans and simmer for a further 30 minutes.

Thicken with the flour or corn flour (corn starch)

Beef and Stout Stew

Serves 8-10

<u>What you will need</u>:

1 litres of rich beef stock

100g of smoked streaky bacon

2 cans of stout

1kg of shin

3 onions

2 knobs of butter

Tablespoon of flour

Flour or cornflour (corn flour) to thicken

<u>What you will need to do</u>:

Dice the shin, roll in the flour and brown in a pan with one nob of the butter. Add to the beef stock, cover and simmer for 2 hours

Dice the onions and finely chop the bacon and fry with the second knob of butter until onions are soft. Add to the stock with the stout and simmer for a further 30 minutes.

Thicken with the flour or corn flour (corn starch)

LAMB STEWS

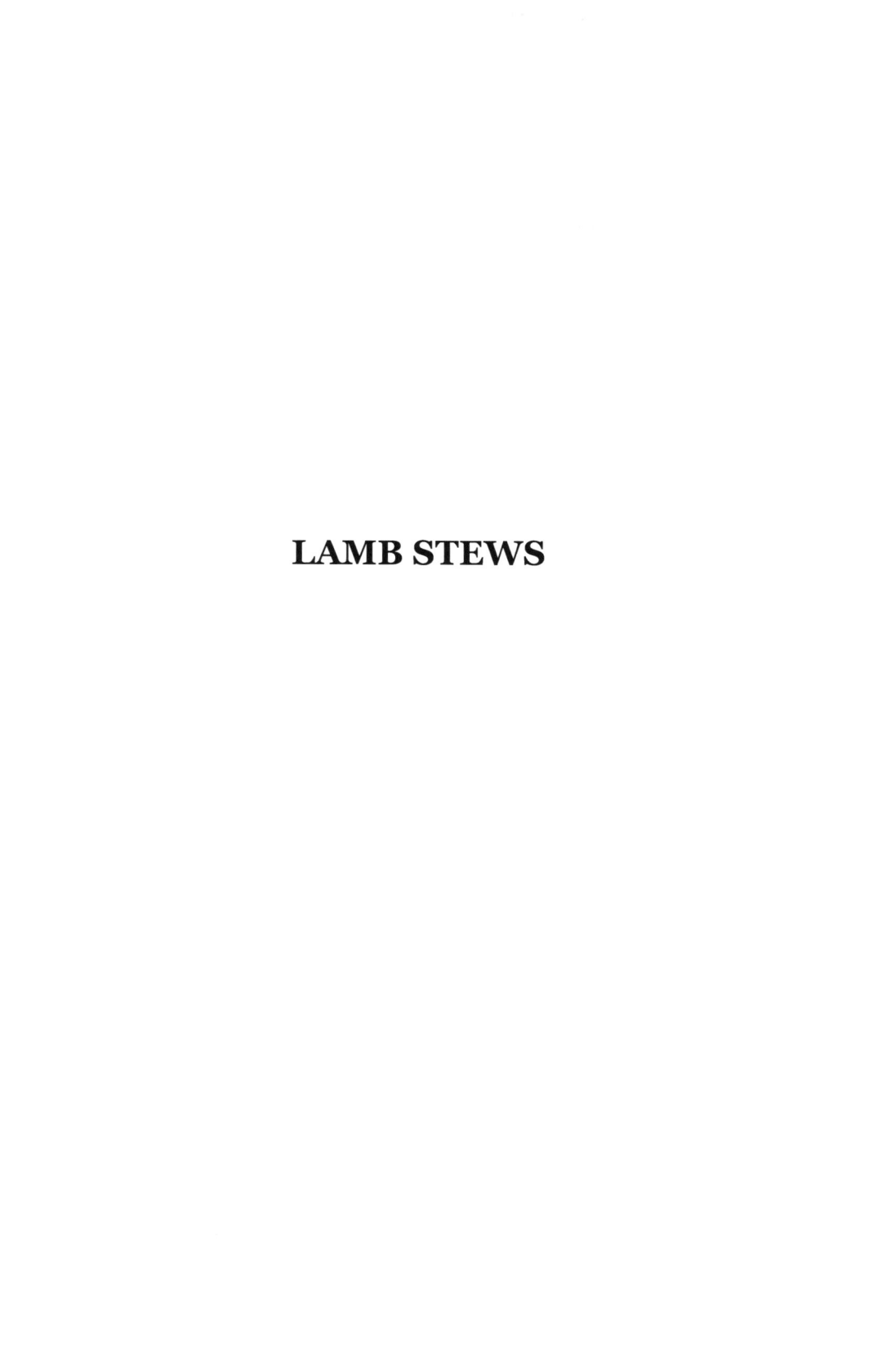

Pan Cooked Gigot and Barley Stew

Serves 6

What you will need:

1 gigot (leg) of mutton

4 carrots

6 white turnips

2 onions

1 litre of your vegetable, brisket and lamb stock

Half a cup of pearl barley

What you will need to do:

Get your butcher to cut the gigot into slices (chops)

Put the chops in a large stew pot and add the stock. Bring to the boil and skim. Simmer gently for 1 hour then add the barley and simmer for a further half an hour.

Chop and dice the carrots, turnip and onions and add to the pot. Simmer for a further hour.

Thicken with flour or corn flour (corn starch)

Lamb and Root Vegetable Stew

Serves 10-12

What you will need:

1 shoulder of lamb

1.5 litres of lamb and vegetable stock

6 potatoes

1 small swede

2 parsnips

6 carrots

6 small white turnips

8 shallots

2 stalks of celery

Half a cup of green lentils

2 knobs of butter

What you will need to do:

Trim the excess fat from the shoulder of lamb and roast the shoulder of lamb in a hot oven for 30 minutes then remove from the oven and add to the stock. Cover and simmer for two and a half hours Chop and dice all of the vegetables (remembering to remove the fibrous, stringy bits from the celery) and fry in a large pan with the butter. Add to the stock after it has simmered for the two and a half hours then rinse and add the lentils and simmer for a further hour. Remove the lamb, 'pull' apart with a fork and add back into the stock

Lamb and Cauliflower Stew

Serves 4-6

What you will need:

500g of lamb shoulder

500mls of lamb and vegetable stock

1 whole small cauliflower (or half of a large cauliflower)

2 onions

2 stalks of celery

4 tomatoes

Tablespoon of flour

2 knobs of butter

What you will need to do:

Remove the excess fat from the lamb and cut into cubes then dust with the flour and brown in a pan with one knob of the butter. Add to the stock, cover and simmer for 2 and a half hours

Dice the onions. Remove the fibrous, stringy bits from the celery and chop then fry off the onions and the celery with the second knob of butter until soft

Blanch, skin and chop the tomatoes. Cut the cauliflower into florets

After the 2 and half hours simmering time, add the onions, celery, tomatoes and cauliflower florets and simmer for a further 30 minutes

Thicken if required with flour or corn flour (corn starch)

Lamb and chickpea Stew

Serves 4-6

What you will need:

500g of lamb shoulder

500mls of lamb and vegetable stock

1 large can of chickpeas

2 stalks of celery

2 onions

1 teaspoon of smoked paprika

2 sprigs of rosemary

1 tablespoon of flour

1 knob of butter

What you will need to do:

Dice the onions and cut up the celery (removing the fibrous stringy bits)

Remove the excess fat from the lamb and cut into cubes. Dust with flour and brown in a pan then add the diced onions and the celery along with the paprika and mix through thoroughly

Add the sprig of rosemary then pour over the stock, cover and simmer for 3 hours

Add the drained tin of chickpeas and simmer for a further 10 minutes. Remove the sprig of rosemary before serving

Lamb Stew with Mint and Peas

Serves 4-6

<u>What you will need</u>:

500g of lamb shoulder

500mls of lamb and vegetable stock

3 cups of frozen garden peas

2 stalks of celery

2 onions

2 tablespoons of fresh mint

2 sprigs of rosemary

1 tablespoon of flour

1 knob of butter

2 tablespoons of chopped parsley

<u>What you will need to do</u>:

Dice the onions and cut up the celery (removing the fibrous stringy bits)

Remove the excess fat from the lamb and cut into cubes. Dust with flour and brown in a pan then add the diced onions and the celery and mix through thoroughly

Add the sprig of rosemary then pour over the stock, cover and simmer for 3 hours

Add the frozen peas and simmer for a further 10 minutes. Finely chop and then add the fresh mint. Remove the sprig of rosemary before serving

Pearl Barley Lamb Shanks (oven cooked)

Serves 4-6

What you will need:

4 lamb shanks

500mls of lamb and vegetable stock

Half a cup of pearl barley

2 onions

1 sprig of rosemary

2 knobs of butter

What you will need to do:

Pre-soak the pearl barley overnight in cold water

Prepare your shanks by removing the outer fibrous skin and then brown in a pan with one of the knobs of butter

Dice the onions and gently soften in a pan with the other knob of butter

Add the shanks and the onions to the stock in a large ovenproof dish then stir in the barley and throw in the rosemary

Cover and cook in the oven on a medium heat for 3 hours

Thicken with flour or cornflour (corn starch)

Remove the rosemary before serving

Spiced lamb Stew

Serves 4-6

What you will need:

500g of lamb shoulder

500mls of lamb and vegetable stock

6 tomatoes

1 tablespoon of tomato puree

Half a teaspoon of cumin

Half a teaspoon of smoked paprika

Half a teaspoon of chilli powder

2 stalks of celery

2 onions

Knob of butter

What you will need to do:

Dice the onions

Remove the excess fat from the lamb and cut into cubes. Dust with flour and brown in a pan then add the diced onions in the along with the spices and mix through thoroughly

Remove the fibrous, stringy bits from the celery, chop and add to the pan Peel and dice the carrots, blanche and skin the tomatoes and roughly chop then add to the pot along with the stock and the tomato puree

Cover and simmer for 3 hours Thicken with flour or corn flour (corn starch

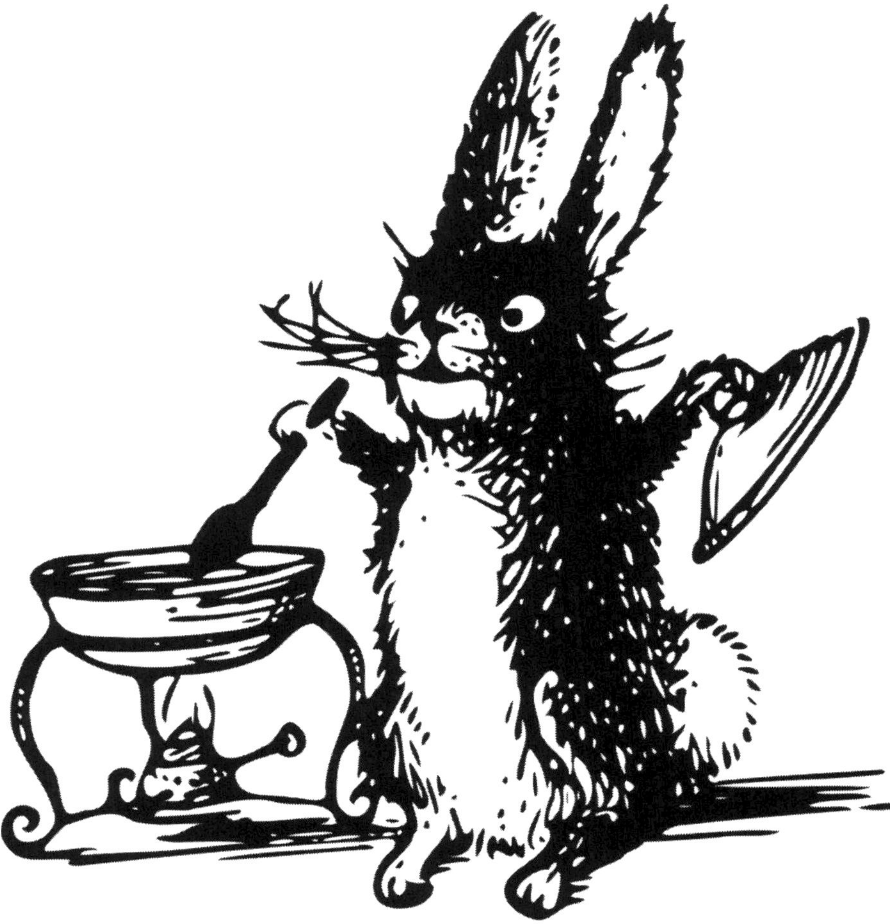

GAME STEWS

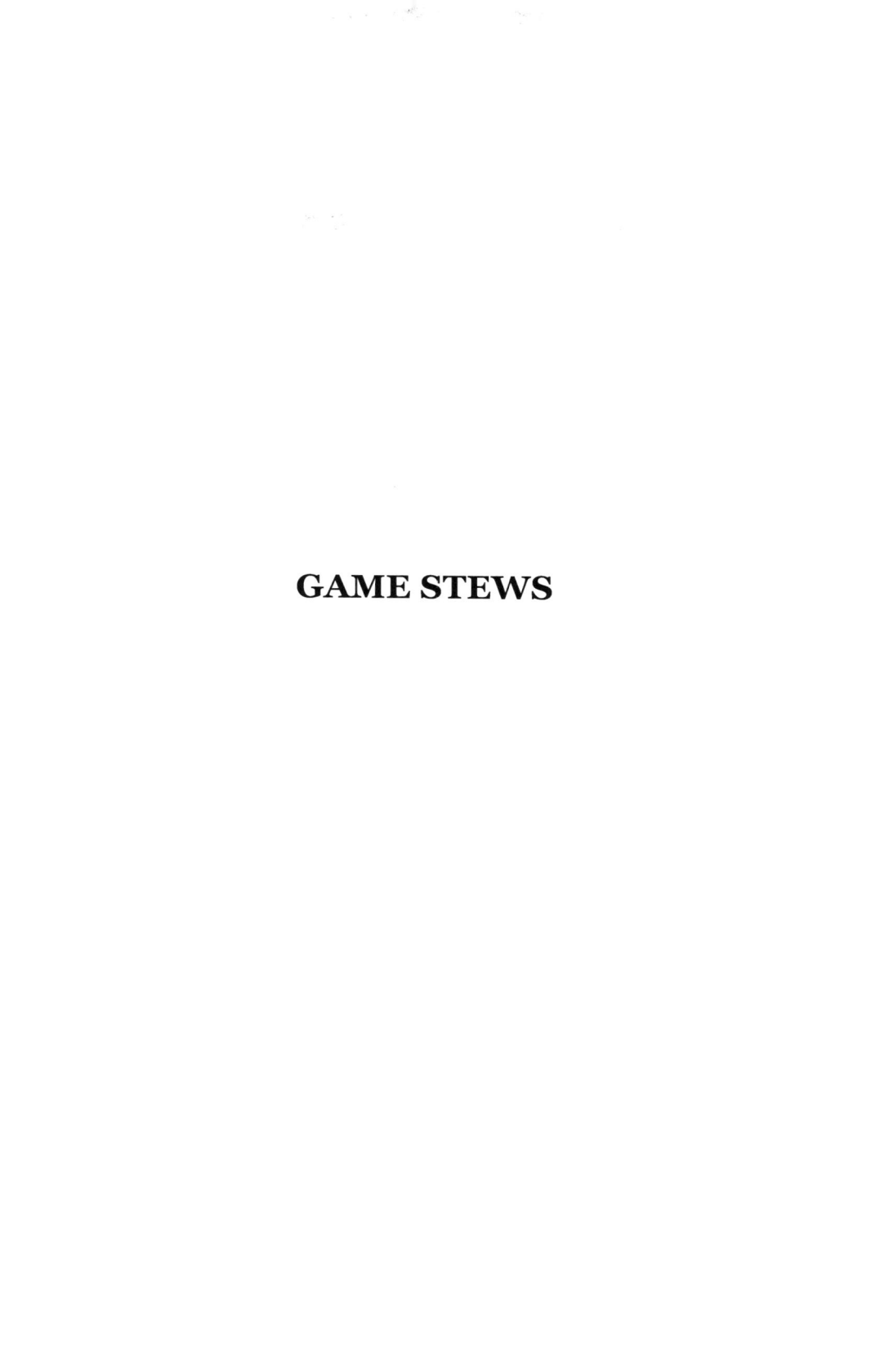

Game Fowl Stew

Serves 8

What you will need:

1 litre of chicken stock

1 partridge

1 small chicken

1 grouse

1 partridge

2 leeks

500g of potatoes

2 carrots

2 sticks of celery

Half a cup of flour

What you will need to do:

Joint all of the birds, dust with flour and fry until golden brown

Chop and dice the potatoes and carrots. Cut the celery into small pieces (having removed the fibrous stringy bits). Cut up the leeks into small pieces. Add the jointed birds and the vegetables to the stock, bring to the boil and then gently simmer for 25 minutes.

Pheasant stew

Serves 4

What you will need:

250mls of chicken stock

1 pheasant

1 tablespoon of flour

1 tablespoon of butter

A half a glass of claret

3 rashers of bacon

Salt and pepper

A tablespoon of chopped flat leaf parsley

What you will need to do:

Joint the bird and dust with flour and fry in the butter until golden brown. Put into a stew pot with the stock and claret. Chop and dice the bacon then add to the pot. Cover and gently simmer for 1 hour.

Garnish with the parsley.

Pheasant stew with cider and bacon (made as a casserole in the oven)

Serves 6

What you will need:

300mls of chicken stock

2 pheasants

100g of bacon

2 apples

2 sticks of celery

Tablespoon of butter

4 sage leaves

500mls of cider

1 savoy cabbage

100mls of cream

What you will need to do:

Pre-heat the oven to 170 degrees C

Melt the butter in a frying pan, season the birds and brown in the pan. Put the birds in an ovenproof dish. Chop the bacon and dice the onion. Cut up the celery (after removing the fibrous stringy bits) and cut up the sage. Add all of these ingredients to the pan and fry gently for 10 minutes, remove excess fat. Cut up the apples and place over the pheasants. Chop the cabbage and add to the dish with the stock and the cider. Cover and put in the oven for 25 minutes then mix the cream through the dish.

Hare Casserole

Serves 4

What you will need:

1 hare (young)

4 rashers of bacon

2 tablespoons of butter

60g (2oz) of flour

500mls of mixed meat stock

3 onions

1 bay leaf

A teaspoon of peppercorns

2 glasses of port

What you will need to do:

Joint the hare and cut the bacon into strips. Chop and dice the onions.

Melt the butter in a frying pan and brown the hare and fry off the bacon. Put into an oven proof dish. Add the stock and stir in the flour, the peppercorns and the bay leaf.

Cover tightly and cook in a slow (low) oven for 3 hours. After 3 hours, stir in the port. Keep the lid off and continue in the oven until the sauce thickens.

Tighnabruaich Rabbit Stew

Serves 4

What you will need:

1 rabbit

30g (1oz) of flour

500mls of mixed meat stock

2 onions

3 carrots

Salt and pepper

1 tablespoon of butter

What you will need to do:

Joint the rabbit

Cut and dice the onions and carrots

Season the flour with salt and pepper and coat the joints of rabbit. and fry in the butter with the carrots and the onions until browned.

Place in a stew pot, cover with the stock and bring to a slow boil. Simmer until tender.

Venison Stew

Serves 4

<u>What you will need</u>:

Half a litre of mixed meat stock

500g of venison shoulder

Knob of butter

2 parsnips

4 potatoes

3 onions

2 cloves of garlic

1 bay leaf

1 teaspoon of celery salt

Tablespoon of flour

<u>What you will need to do:</u>

Cube the venison and dust with the flour then brown in the butter. Add to the stock, cover and simmer for one and a half hours

Peel and chop the parsnips and the onions and mince the garlic

Peel and cube the potatoes and then add all of the vegetables with the celery salt and the bay leaf to the pot and cook for a further 20 minutes

Remove the bay leaf and thicken if required with flour

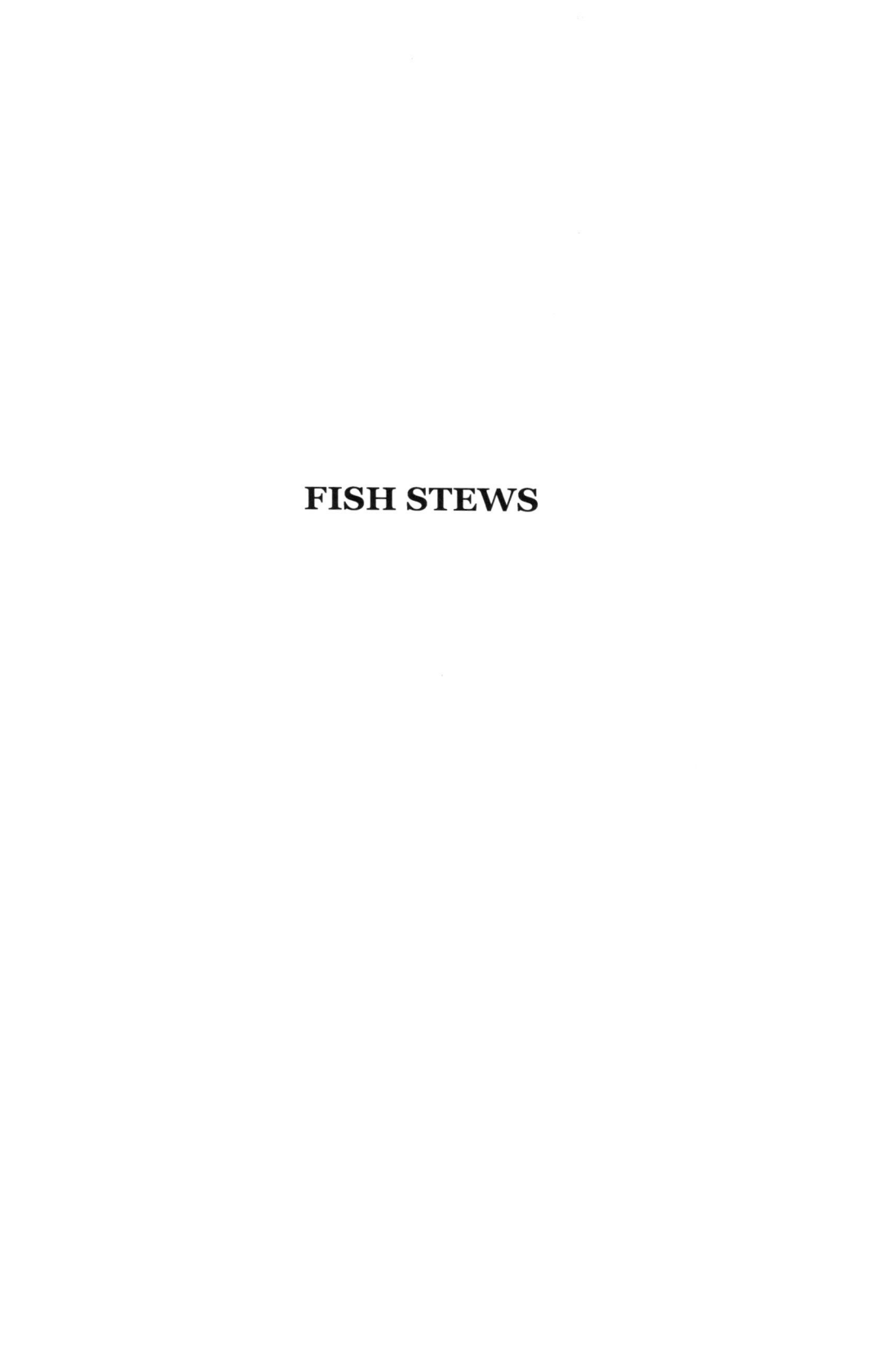

FISH STEWS

Creamy Tomato Fish Stew

Serves 4

<u>What you will need</u>:

1 cup of basic fish stock

200g of cod fillet

200g of haddock (or whiting) fillet

4 tomatoes

Half a teaspoon of celery salt

1 cup of cream

<u>What you will need to do:</u>

Blanche, skin and chop the tomatoes and put in a pan with the stock. Add the celery salt and, uncovered, simmer for 10 minutes and then add the cream (stir, ensuring the cream doesn't split) and simmer uncovered for a further 5 minutes

Skin and cube the fish and add to the pot. Simmer for a further 5 minutes

Whiting Stew with Leeks and Bacon

Serves 4

What you will need:

1 cup of basic fish stock

8 whiting fillets

1 large leek

1 stalk of celery

2 rashers of lean smoky bacon

1 potato

1 carrot

1 tablespoon of parsley

1 knob of butter

1 teaspoon of vegetable oil

What you will need to do:

Peel and cube the potato and cook in the fish stock until soft then mash to thicken the stock

Wash and finely chop the leek. Remove the fibrous, stringy bits from the celery and finely chop. Dice the lean bacon and fry until crispy in the vegetable oil. Meantime, fry off the leeks and celery in the butter until soft. Add the bacon, leeks and celery to the potato and stock and bring back to a gentle simmer (add more stock if required)

Add the fish and simmer for 10 minutes. Chop the parsley and add just before serving

Luxury Fish Stew

Serves 6

What you will need:

1 cup of the rich shellfish stock

1 cup of cream

200g of skinned cod fillet

200g of skinned haddock (or whiting) fillet

200g of prawns

1 lobster tail

2 skinned salmon fillets

1 onion

1 clove of garlic

1 bulb of fennel

1 knob of butter

2 tablespoons of chopped coriander

What you will need to do:

Dice the onion, crush the garlic and finely slice the fennel and fry until soft with the knob of butter.

Skin and cube the white fish. Cut the lobster tail into 6 pieces, Cut each salmon fillet into 3 pieces.

Bring your stock to a gentle simmer and add the onions and fennel. Add the lobster tail. Simmer for 1 minute and then add the cubed white fish and the salmon. Simmer for a further minute and then add the prawns and the cream and simmer for 2 minutes. Thicken with flour or cornflour (corn starch) if required and add the chopped coriander before serving

Spicy Fish Stew

Serves 4

What you will need:

4 skinned salmon fillets

200g of prawns

1 cup of basic fish stock

2 cloves of garlic

1 onion

200g of red kidney beans

4 tomatoes

1 potato

Half a teaspoon of chilli powder

Half a teaspoon of turmeric

Half a teaspoon of ground ginger

Half a teaspoon of cumin

Half a cup of cream

A tablespoon of chopped coriander

Knob of butter

What you will need to do:

Peel and finely dice the potatoes. Dice the onion and slice the garlic and add everything to a pan with the butter and fry until soft. Add the spices and mix through thoroughly

Blanche, skin and chop the tomatoes and add to the stock along with the spiced potatoes, onions and garlic. Simmer for 10 minutes and then add the kidney beans and the fish

Simmer for a further 5 minutes and then stir in the cream. Simmer for a further 5 minutes

Add the coriander just before serving

Fish Stew with Garlic and Butterbeans

Serves 4

<u>What you will need:</u>

1 cup of basic fish stock

1 onion

200g of skinned cod fillets

200g of skinned haddock (or whiting fillets)

1 large can (400g) of butterbeans

1 whole garlic bulb

2 stalks of celery

Half a cup of frozen garden peas

Teaspoon of vegetable oil

Knob of butter

1 teaspoon of dill

<u>What you will need to do:</u>

Rub the vegetable oil into the bulb of garlic, wrap in tinfoil and roast for 30 minutes in a hot oven.

Dice the onions and chop the celery and fry until soft in the butter

When the garlic has roasted sufficiently to allow you to squeeze it out of the cloves, add the garlic to the onions and celery and then mix through the frozen peas. Add this mixture to the fish stock and simmer for 10 minutes

Cube the fish and add to the pan and simmer for a further 5 minutes then add the butterbeans and continue simmering for a further 5 minutes

Add the dill just before serving

A word from the author

Thank you for your interest in my wee granny's recipes. I hope you get many years of enjoyment in cooking and eating them.

If you enjoyed My Wee Granny's Soups and Stews, please consider rating and reviewing on Amazon or Goodreads

For more books by the author, please visit

https://angelahossackbooks.com

Printed in Great Britain
by Amazon